True Identity

{{Let's Strengthen Our Character Together}}

Written By Davon Hubbard

Contents

Acknowledgments   7

Introduction   9

Chapter 2 - Feelings   20

Chapter 3 - Be Mindful   34

Chapter 4 - WHO ARE YOU, At any rate?   40

Chapter 5 - Pen and Paper Required   47

Chapter 6 - What Is Character?   50

Chapter 7 - How Does Personality Impact Connections?   57

Chapter 8 - The Battle is First in Our Minds   60

Chapter 9 - David and Goliath   66

Chapter 10 - Your Character Is a Key Front Line   69

Chapter 11 - Our Undeniable Personality   76

Chapter 12 - Ways to Adapt to a Personality Emergency   88

Chapter 13 - Review   90

Chapter 14 – Gender Identity   98

Chapter 15 - Step-by-step instructions to be consistent with yourself   103

Understanding Your Emotions/Feelings   110

Sources   115

About the Author   116

Acknowledgments

To all the times I forgot to say thank you, or said it in a way that didn't quite compute and conveyed how much my mom means to me - for always being there no matter what and listening attentively when words fail me. Mom, for imparting on me great life skills such as compassion, altruism and kindness; I want to say thank you and I love you. You have been so special to me over the years, more than you know. Knowing all this makes saying thank you seem almost petty by comparison but please know that every act of kindness and love I have great appreciation for, it's not only acknowledged but felt deeply within my heart. There isn't one thing you do for me that doesn't touch some deep tender spot inside of me - from your patience with dealing with an ungrateful child (especially during hard parenting moments), being there through thick and thin even when we were worlds apart despite obstacles...I am grateful beyond measure! And most importantly, thank you for your love and support. I love you Mom!

Introduction

If you want to move from where you are to where you want to be, you need to create a new identity. Notwithstanding, taking on "another you" is troublesome if you feel as though you've lost your personality. Even though it may appear as though it would be ideal to fill the void; however, first, you must locate yourself before you can recreate yourself.

It makes sense that it can sometimes be challenging to identify your true self. The false identity is the critical voice in your head, which the Bible refers to as "the natural man." Your genuine identity is the divine character of who God made you to be. In today's society of comparison, self-deprecation, and social media idolatry, it's simple to get buried in your false identity and lose sight of who you really are. But beyond the layers of society's expectations, the roles you perform, and the messages you have been given, you will find your entire, wonderful, and deserving self.

With identity politics, a wide range of gender identification possibilities, "selfies," and a "you-do-you" mentality, society emphasizes individualism. Still, people seem to find it more difficult than ever to define who they are. They are looking for their identity in the wrong places, which is the problem.

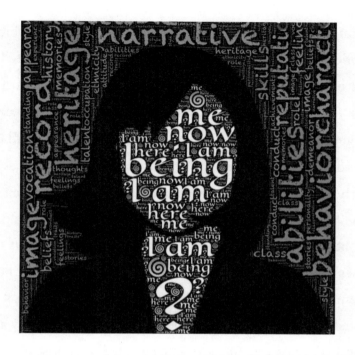

A young girl named Anonima Marie Camila Vega grew up feeling a bit neglected as a child because her parents partied all the time. And when they weren't partying, her father physically and mentally abused her mother. All this young girl wanted was to feel loved. She acted out, but they were too busy to notice.

She took a different approach. She went to the church at the corner of her block. Anonima loved the attention she got from the pastor and the Sunday school teachers so much that she began to have these crazy feelings about them. Watching her parents getting high and sleeping with each other was what she believed to be normal. She would hear the bible stories about loving one another, which would get twisted in her mind because of all the things she had seen and heard in her younger years. She became very promiscuous and eager to get anyone's attention. When she was rejected or heard the word 'No,' it only meant to try harder, she was taught at an early age to manipulate any situation to get what she wanted. She realized later in life that those skills had become a part of her genetic make-up, her identity. She has blurred the lines of truth and lies with her fake realities; she couldn't tell them apart. She became abusive toward guys she liked or dated because she refused to become a victim and show any signs of weakness. She knew she wanted to be just like her father, strong and adored by all. He had a silver tongue; he could sweet-talk anyone and make you do what he wanted.

Our most significant convictions are those we hold about our identity. Individuals have colossal capacities for the past's thought process to be conceivable. The ability to take advantage of our enormous expectations comes from our character: how we characterize ourselves and what we accept we can accomplish.

Identity is the most grounded force in human character. We have a profound standing need to stay predictable with how we characterize ourselves. Any change you make inside yourself will rely upon your capacity to grow as a person. By building a new, enabling arrangement of convictions, you can make an enduring change inside and in your life.

Personality is the main power that decides our activities. We will act as indicated by our perspectives on who we really are — regardless of whether these perspectives are precise. When we know what our identity is, we will be able to figure out how to act naturally. Attempting to live in a manner that conflicts with our real essence will make the existence of dissatisfaction, stress, and frustration. We should figure out how to embrace our most profound requirements, wants, qualities, fears, values, and convictions to make an agreement and tap into our enormous potential.

The young lady viewed her family as dysfunctional, functional addicts. They got up every day after partying all night and went to work. You can't get high if you can't afford it. So, their work ethic was great; they worked hard and partied even harder. It gave you a view of work-life balance. One day, Anonima decided she would see the big deal and try this white line. It looked so pretty on this unicorn board; she knew what to do because she would watch everyone sniffing this powder by holding a nostril or rolling up a dollar bill from the basement steps. So, one morning while she was getting ready for school, she mustered enough courage to do a line. She put that board to her nose and took a big sniff; it made her feel dizzy, and her heart started to race. She heard a noise that sounded like someone was coming into the house, so she hid in the closet. It sounded like a woman was with her dad.

No one noticed that Anonima's school bag was on the back of the chair and that she didn't go to school or wasn't seen all day long. The day went on as it always did. About 36 hours later, she woke up in that closet feeling confused, unaware of how she ended up in the closet, but finally, it came to her that she had snorted that line of cocaine. It made her feel like she had been asleep for weeks. She felt a little sad because no one noticed she was missing, not even her siblings.

Individuals sometimes keep up with the deception that their way of behaving determines who they truly are. Nothing could be further from reality. We have all accomplished snapshots of uneasiness and root and subsequently have said or done things that don't reflect our identity. It doesn't make these ways of behaving a piece of our character. Rather, they are transitory breaches or novel endeavors to address our issues at the time. At the point when you assume liability, you reestablish your personality. When we cause negative or unfriendly circumstances, we ought to make a move to fix any mischief we might have caused. The quickest method for growing our character is accomplishing something conflicting with our mental self-view. For instance, complete a test like ziplining or sky plunging as a method for making a splash. Our own characters are in a consistent condition of development. We can reevaluate ourselves and make a new, engaging personality that grows with what is conceivable in our lives. The key is to assume cognizant command over our convictions about ourselves, so they can move us toward what we want most. As it's been said, the type of food you eat will affect your general health; the equivalent goes with your opinion of yourself. Your negative considerations will reflect in your present status of the brain, which will show by the way you view yourself.

Anonima felt unloved and unwanted. Her brothers always teased her and told her that they found her in the trash can, and that's how she felt like discarded trash. She thought about how stupid she was to do that drug because she could have died, but they probably wouldn't have noticed till her body started to rot. Just imagine that would have blown their high. They would have gone to jail; her brother would have ended up in foster care or with a relative. Or she could have overdosed and ended up in the hospital, but God had his hand on her to keep her safe and to have her just sleep it off. That one event could have ruined everyone's life.

You and I need to prepare ourselves for change. You and I need to turn into our own advocates. Once more, we face our own lives. We will choose to make those long-haul changes and be liable for our own change, not any other person, just you.

First, we should accept, "Something should change" — not that it ought to change, not that it could or should, but that it totally should. So frequently, I hear individuals say, "This weight ought to fall off," "Tarrying is a crummy propensity," or "My connections ought to be better." Yet you know, we can "ought to" all over ourselves; our life won't change! When something turns into a must, we start genuinely doing what's important to move the nature of our lives.

Second, we should accept that things should change; however, we should accept, "I should change it." We should consider ourselves to be the wellspring of change. If not, we'll constantly be searching for another person to roll out the improvements for us, and we'll continuously have another person to blame when it doesn't end up working. We should be the wellspring of our change if our change will endure.

Third, we want to accept, "I can transform it." Without trusting that it's feasible as far as we're concerned to change, as we've proactively talked about, we have no possibility of helping through our cravings. Without these three center convictions, I can guarantee you that any change you make has a decent potential for success of being over in a short while. Kindly don't misjudge me — it's dependably savvy to get an extraordinary mentor (a specialist, a guide, somebody who's as of now delivered these outcomes for the majority of others) to help you in finding a way, the legitimate ways to overcome your fear or quit smoking or get more fit. Be that as it may; eventually, you must be the wellspring of your change.

Ask yourself what you genuinely need throughout your everyday life. Do you need a caring marriage and the admiration of your kids? Do you need a lot of cash, quick vehicles, a flourishing business, and a house on the top of

17

the mountain? Would you like to venture to the far corners of the earth, visit colorful ports of call, and see verifiable milestones firsthand? Maybe you should ask yourself, "For what reason do I need these things?" Don't you need fine vehicles, for instance, since you truly want the sensations of achievement and eminence you figure they could bring? For what reason do you need an extraordinary everyday life? Is it since you figure it will give you sensations of adoration, closeness, association, or warmth? To put it plainly, then, at that point, isn't it genuine that what you truly need is essentially a meaningful impact on the way you feel? All that matters is your desired truth, these things or results, since you consider them to be a way to accomplish specific sentiments, feelings, or states you want. When someone kisses you, what encourages you at that time? Is it wet tissue contacting wet tissue that truly sets off the inclination? Obviously not! Assuming that is valid, kissing your canine would turn you on!

Our feelings are all only a whirlwind of biochemical tempests in our cerebrums — and we can start them without warning. In any case, we should first figure out how to assume command over them deliberately instead of living in response. The vast majority of our close-to-home reactions are learned reactions to the climate. We've purposely demonstrated some of them and coincidentally found others.

Chapter 2 - Feelings

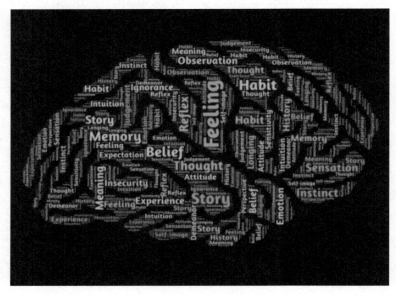

Anonima continued playing outside, running the streets, and doing odd jobs to get money. She sold cake slices, cleaned houses except her own, babysat kids, sold friendship bracelets, sold broken toys, and organized junk anything to make a dollar. She was resilient. This little girl was ten years old when she came into womanhood, and the first thing she wanted to do was tell her mom that she was bleeding and didn't know why. She thought she had cut herself. She picked up the phone to call her mom, but she wouldn't answer because, by that time, she had left her daughter behind to pursue another man. So, when her mom didn't answer, she went to the neighbor's house and told her what was happening to her body. She gave her the birds and the bees story and showed her how to protect herself and keep clean. Anonima's mother didn't call back for three days, and she left several messages. This young lady was very sad, but she finally told her dad what was happening. He gave her money and said go ask the neighbor to get what you need. That next day Anonima's dad was so high, and he wanted Anonima to call her mother, so she picked up the phone and called, but there was no answer; he made her call repeatedly. He got so angry that he took the old heavy rotary phone and cracked her right above the eye, and the blood started pouring out. It took a while for it to stop bleeding. She ran to the neighbors for help to stop the bleeding; they put butterfly stitches on it. Anonima's father's high started to wear off; later, he apologized and gave her money to forget. Later that week, he organized a big party, and everyone was high and drunk; someone even tried to come into her room. She would sleep really hard and would pee in the bed because of that, but thankfully that night, she was soaked, and when this man attempted to pull her clothes off her, the smell made him sick, and he left the room, but I think it was because she told him that she was going to tell. It was dark, and she couldn't see who the man was. Afterward, she put the chair in front of the door so no one else could sneak into her room.

When Anonima finally spoke with her mother, she begged her to come to save her, saying that it wasn't safe anymore, that dad hit her and that he wanted Anonima to be just like her mother, a servant, maid, cook, and a punching bag. So, she said, "OK, I'll pick you up on the Ave. at the bus stop." So Anonima packed up a trash bag of clothes and proceeded to run away to her mother on the Ave. She was excited; she waited all day long until it got dark and had to walk back home because her mom didn't show up. She felt totally abandoned after she found out it was her boyfriend who stopped her from coming.

LOVE AND WARMTH.

The predictable articulation of affection is by all accounts ready to liquefy practically any negative feelings it interacts with. Assuming somebody is angry with you, you can undoubtedly stay adoring with them by embracing a center conviction like this glorious one from this book. All correspondence is either a caring reaction or a weep for help. Assuming somebody comes to you in a condition of harm or outrage, and you reliably answer them with adoration and warmth, in the long run, their state will change, and their force will liquefy away.

APPRECIATION

I accept that the most remarkable feelings are all some articulation of adoration, each coordinating differently. As far as I might be concerned, appreciation is the most otherworldly feeling, effectively offering through viewpoint and activity my appreciation and love for all the gifts that life has given me, that individuals have given me, and that experience has given me. Living in this profound state will upgrade your life more than nearly anything I am aware of. Developing this is developing life. Live with a mentality of appreciation.

INTEREST

If you truly have any desire to fill in your life, figure out how to be pretty much as inquisitive as a kid. Kids know step-by-step instructions to ponder — that is why they're so charming. To fix fatigue, be interested. Assuming you're inquisitive, nothing is a task; it's programmed — you need to study. Develop interest, and life turns into a ceaseless investigation of euphoria.

FERVOR & ENTHUSIASM

Zeal and enthusiasm can add juice to anything. Energy can turn any test into a colossal open door. Enthusiasm is an unrestrained ability to push our lives ahead at a quicker beat than at any time in recent memory. How would we "get" energy? In the same way, we "get" love, warmth, appreciation, thankfulness, and interest — we choose to feel it! Utilize your physiology: talk even more quickly, envision pictures more quickly, and move your body where you need to head. Try not to simply nonchalantly sit and think. You can't be loaded up with energy assuming that you're stooping over your work area, breathing shallowly, and slurring your discourse.

ASSURANCE

The above feelings are all significant, yet there is one that you should have if you want to make enduring worthwhile in this world. It will direct how you manage difficulties and challenges, with dissatisfaction and bafflement. Assurance implies distinguishing between being stuck and being hit with the lightning force of responsibility. If you have any desire to inspire yourself to get thinner, settle on those business decisions, or finish anything, "propelling" yourself will not make it happen. Placing yourself in a condition of assurance will. Every one of your activities will spring from that source, and you'll just naturally take the necessary steps to achieve your objective. Acting with assurance implies making a harmonious, serious choice where you've removed some other chance. Earnestly, you can achieve anything. Without it, you're unfortunate to dissatisfaction and frustration. Our ability to take the necessary steps, to act notwithstanding dread, is the foundation of courage.

What's more, mental resilience is the establishment from which assurance is conceived. The contrast between accomplishment and sadness is the development of the close-to-home muscle of assurance. Why crush through a wall on the off chance you can simply look a little to one side and track down an entryway? Here and there, assurance can be a restriction; you really want to develop . . .

ADAPTABILITY

Assuming there's one seed to establish that will ensure a positive outcome, it's the capacity to change your approach. As a matter of fact, every one of those Activity

Signs — those things you used to call gloomy feelings — are simply messages to be more adaptable! Deciding to be adaptable is deciding to be content. All through your life, there will be times when there are things you cannot handle, and your capacity to be adaptable in your guidelines, the importance you connect to things and your activities will decide your drawn-out progress or disappointment, also your degree of individual bliss. On the off chance that you develop the above feelings in general, you'll clearly create...

CERTAINTY

Unfaltering certainty is the feeling of belief that we as a whole care about. The main way you can reliably encounter certainty, even in conditions and circumstances you've never beforehand experienced, is through the force of confidence. Envision and have a specific outlook on the feelings you have the right to have now, instead of sitting tight for them to unexpectedly show up sometime or another in the far-off future. When you're certain, you're willing to try, to risk yourself. One method for creating confidence and certainty is to utilize it. If I somehow happened to find out that you're sure you can tie your shoes, I'm certain you could perceive me with amazing certainty that you would be able.

Why? Simply because you've done it so many times! So, practice certainty by utilizing it reliably, and you'll be amazed at the profits it yields in each part of your life. The capacity to follow up on trust pushes mankind ahead. One more inclination you'll naturally encounter whenever you've prevailed regarding developing all the above is …

LIVELINESS

At the point when I added liveliness to my rundown of most significant qualities, people would say, "there's something else about you. You appear to be so cheerful." I understood that I had been blissful; however, I didn't refine my face! There's a major contrast between being cheerful within and being obviously bright. Brightness upgrades your confidence, makes life more interesting and makes individuals around you feel more joyful also. Happiness can dispose of the sensations of dread, hurt, outrage, dissatisfaction, frustration, discouragement, responsibility, and deficiency in your life.

You accomplish liveliness the day you understand that regardless of what's going on around you, being something besides happy won't improve it. Being bright doesn't imply that you're Pollyanna or that you only choose

27

to look at the good in everything and deny recognizing difficulties. Being bright means, you're amazingly smart because you know that on the off chance that you carry on with life in a condition of delight — one that is serious to such an extent that you communicate a feeling of euphoria to people around you as I've learned in my Buddhist practice — you can address any difficulty that comes to your direction. Develop happiness, and you won't require so many of those "excruciating" Activity Signs to stand out! Cause it's simple for yourself to feel merry by sowing the seed of…

IMPERATIVENESS

It is important to deal with this area. On the off chance that you don't deal with your actual body, it's more difficult to have the option to partake in these feelings. Ensure that actual essentialness is accessible; recall that all feelings are coordinated through your body. If you're feeling upset deeply, you want to check out the nuts and bolts. How are you relaxing? When individuals are worried, they quit breathing, draining their imperativeness.

Figuring out how to inhale appropriately is the main road toward great wellbeing. Another key component, actual essentialness, guarantees that you have a plentiful degree of nerve energy. How would you do this? Understand that every day you're consuming nerve energy through your activities, and as clear as it sounds, you, in all reality, do have to ensure that you rest and re-energize. By the way, how much rest would you say you are getting? Assuming you're routinely getting eight to ten hours of sack time, you're most likely getting excessive rest! Six to seven hours has been viewed as ideal for the vast majority. The human sensory system needs to move to have energy. Partially, consuming energy provides you with a more noteworthy feeling of energy. As you move, oxygen courses through your body, and that actual degree of wellbeing make the profound feeling of imperativeness that can help you with managing essentially any negative challenge you could have in your life, so understand that a feeling of essentialness is an important feeling to develop to deal with feelings that surface in your life. Also the basic asset in encountering steady energy. When your nursery is loaded up with these strong feelings, then you can share your abundance through.

COMMITMENT

"What do I really want to do to turn my life around?" Suddenly an understanding came to me, followed by an extraordinary feeling that I was forced to note down one vital expression in my diary: "The key to living is giving." There could be no more extravagant feeling I am aware of in life than the feeling that your identity, something you've said or done, has added to something other than your own life, that in some way it has upgraded valuable's insight for somebody you care about. Or perhaps for somebody you don't have the slightest idea about. The stories that move me most significantly are about individuals who follow the most remarkable thoughtful feeling of caring genuinely and acting for others' advantage. When I saw the melodic Les Misérables, I was profoundly moved by the personality of Jean Valjean since he was a decent man who needed to give such a huge amount to other people. Every day we should develop that feeling of commitment by zeroing in on ourselves and others too.

Try not to fall into the snare of attempting to add to others on your own — playing the saint won't provide you with a genuine feeling of commitment. Yet, suppose there is a possibility that you can reliably provide for yourself furthermore on a quantifiable scale that permits you to realize that your life has made a difference. In that case, you'll have a feeling of association with individuals and a deep satisfaction and confidence that no measure of cash, achievements, acclaim, or affirmation might at any point give. A feeling of commitment makes all of life advantageous. Envision what a superior world it would be if we all developed a feeling of commitment!

You could ask, "Doesn't my experience restrict my personality?" No, it's restricted by your translation of your experience. Your character is only the choices you've made about your identity and what you've chosen to intertwine yourself with. You become the names you've given yourself. The way you characterize your personality characterizes your life.

It doesn't take an emergency for the greater part of us to understand that we can change our behavior; however, the possibility of changing our character appears to be undermining or difficult to most. Splitting away from our center convictions about our identity gives us the most extreme aggravation. Certain individuals would try and venture to such an extreme as to kill themselves to protect those convictions. It was represented in Victor Hugo's magnum opus Les Misérables. At the point when the legend Jean Valjean is let out of his jail work group, he is disappointed and alone. Albeit in the numerous years he's spent in the care of the French police, he has never acknowledged his name of "criminal" (he'd just taken a portion of bread to take care of his needy family and was condemned to numerous long stretches of really difficult work), once delivered, he finds that he can't get a decent living. He is hated and repelled, given his status as an ex-convict.

At long last, in a condition of defenselessness, he starts to acknowledge the personality that his cultural name has forced. He then becomes a lawbreaker and starts to go about in that capacity. Truth be told, when a caring minister takes him in, takes care of him, and gives him cover for the evening, he satisfies his criminal character by taking his advocate's modest silverware. At the point when the police stop Valjean on a standard check, they find that he is an ex-convict. Yet, again he is conveying the minister's most significant belongings — a wrongdoing deserving of an existence of really difficult work. Valjean is taken back to confront the minister, an endless supply of current realities; that's what the cleric demands. The silver was a gift and reminded Valjean that he's failed to remember the two excess silver candles. To Valjean's further shock, the minister consequently makes his liberal deception a reality and sends him away with the silver to begin another life.

Valjean needs to manage the minister's activities. How could he trust him? For what reason didn't he send him away in chains? The cleric let him know that he was his sibling and that Valjean presently did not have a place with evil. He was a genuine man and an offspring of God. This huge event hinders Valjean's character. He destroys his jail papers, moves to another city, and expects another personality. As he does, his behavior changes; he becomes a pioneer and helps those locally.

Nonetheless, a cop, Monsieur Javert, makes it his life's campaign to track down Valjean and bring him to equity. He "knows" Valjean is detestable and characterizes himself as one who deals with evil. When Javert finally finds him, Valjean has the chance to dispense with his foe — yet he unselfishly extras his life. After a long pursuit, Javert finds that Valjean is a decent man — maybe a preferred man over him — and he can't understand that perhaps he was the brutal and evil throne. Subsequently, he hurls himself entirely into the rapids of the stream.

Chapter 3 - Be Mindful

Now 10 was a defining year for her. She had a neighbor who would play the guitar and sing silly songs to get all the kids to hang out with him. He even took her to Jerry's Corner and let Anonima drive his car. One day she noticed him from her bedroom window walking around the room naked. She couldn't believe what she saw. She called her best friend to come over and see; they laughed and teased each other, making jokes. The next day he did it again, but this time he saw her peeking in the window; he smiled and continued what he was doing. She thought maybe he didn't see her. Anonima would go outside and sell friendship bracelets, and the music man would buy a lot of them; he would buy anything she would sell. He would play his guitar and sing silly songs using names like "Banana-Fana Fo Fana Fee fi Mo manna Banana'. The kids would laugh, and he would set some of the kids on his lap to play the guitar. He had a daughter, Sally, who came once a month to visit him, so she would come over to play. She was having a sleepover for her birthday, and only five girls were invited. Sally said that Anonima and her best friend could come along with her cousin and one of her friends. Anonima's dad gave her permission for the sleepover. He didn't know where they were going, and neither did they. We all got in the car and drove off, it felt like they had been in the car for hours, but the girls were busy talking and not paying attention to where they were going.

Finally, they arrived at this boarded-up house with newspaper on the windows and cobwebs everywhere. The kitchen had old cans of food, and everything was dirty and dusty. Anonima and her best friend were scared; it was in a creepy house.

Kids being kids, tried to make the best out of the situation by telling ghost stories and having pillow fights in the living room on the sofa bed. The music man was upstairs while they were playing. Later he would call each girl up one at a time; they would hear the TV playing what sounded like porn. Anonima and her best friend made a plan that when he would call one of them, they would go together. The girls heard crying and muffled screams. They were terrified; finally, he called Anonima, and they both went up the stairs holding each other's hand. When they got in the room, he was naked and wanted them to come close and watch TV with him, just as they suspected it was porn on the TV. Anonima told him her dad would kill him if he knew the music man was trying to get them to watch porn while he did not have his clothes on. So, he thought about it and said he was just testing them to see if they would do it and said they passed the test and gave them $20.00 a piece to not mention this game. They took the money and went back downstairs. His daughter and the other two girls all came down crying and scared.

Anonima and her best friend got in bed scared because what if he tried doing something again the next day? The girls didn't say what happened when they were up in his room, but it was an unspoken sound that you will never forget.

Anonima and her friend held each other all night to keep one another safe. They had one night to get through. The mood was sad; everyone kept to themselves, not saying a word. Later that evening, he called them up again. This time Anonima and her friend tried to open the door to leave, but there was a padlock on it, and every window was locked and covered with newspaper, so they couldn't see anything. It was dark all day there. Anonima acted like her stomach was hurting and asked to go home, so he didn't attempt again. The next morning, he took everyone home and acted like nothing was wrong. Later that evening, he was out on the porch playing the guitar again. That Monday afternoon, the cops arrested him for raping those girls. Afterward, Anonima and her best friend got questioned by their parents and the police. This situation could have been so much worse; sad for the young girls who were molested, but he could have kept them trapped there longer, or he could have killed them. If Anonima didn't tell him her dad would kill him, he might not have cared and done what he wanted to do. She was brave enough to speak up and acknowledge the fear of someone stronger than them, which is what helped her. He told her he knew she was looking in the window; he said, "why look when you can touch." That sick bastard took advantage of those kids gaining their trust and stealing their innocence.

In all the world, there is no other person precisely like me. All that emerges from me is truly mine since I alone picked it - - I own every little thing about me: my body, my sentiments, my mouth, my voice, every one of my activities, whether they be to other people or myself. I own my dreams, fantasies, expectations, and apprehensions. I own my victories and triumphs, every one of my disappointments and missteps. Since I own every bit of myself, I can become personally familiar with myself. Thus, I can cherish myself and be agreeable with every one of my parts. I realize there are perspectives about myself that puzzle me and different perspectives that I don't have the slightest idea about - - yet; for however long I am cordial and wanting of myself, I can bravely and ideally search for answers for the riddles and ways of figuring out more about me. Anyway, I look and sound, anything I say and do, and anything I think and feel at a given time is genuinely me. Assuming later a few pieces of what I looked like, sounded, thought, and got a handle on got to be ill-suited, I can dispose of that which is unsuitable, keep the rest, and create a new thing for myself. I can see, hear, feel, think, say, and do. I have the apparatus to get by, to be near others, to be useful, and to check out and arrange out of the millions of people and things beyond me. I own myself, and in this way, I can design myself. I'm me, and I'm OK.

You can encounter any of these by altering how you utilize your body! You can have areas of strength for feeling, smile, and transform anything in a moment by simply chuckling. You've heard the familiar saying, "Sometime in the not-so-distant future; you'll think back on this and giggle." Assuming that is valid, why not think back and smile now? Why wait? Wake your body up; figure out how to reliably place it in pleasurable states, regardless. How? Build strength by considering something repeatedly, and you'll change the sensations and connect to that situation later. If you utilize your body in weak ways, assuming you drop your shoulders consistently and stroll around like you're drained, you will feel tired. How is it that you could do in any case? Your body drives your feelings. The close-to-home state you're in then starts to influence your body, turning into a kind of perpetual circle. Notice how you're sitting even at this point. Sit up this moment and put more energy into your body as you proceed not exclusively to pursue yet in addition to dominating these standards.

Chapter 4 - WHO ARE YOU, At any rate?

When Anonima was 12, she finally went to stay with her mom, but she didn't really have a stable living situation, so she and her boyfriend stayed with Anonima's cousin in the projects. She was not exactly where she wanted to be, but she was happy to have her mom back in her life. Anonima's uncle was in and out of rehab, battling with his addiction, so he would hang out there too. But one night, he got high and tried to steal her innocence. He came into the room where she was sleeping and pulled her wet panties off her; if it wasn't for the cool breeze, she probably wouldn't have woken up; all she could say was, "stop. I don't want to." Once more, she was thankful that she had wet the bed. The next morning, she went to her mom and told her that Unk had pulled her panties off, and they confronted him. Since then, they didn't see him for like eight years. She thought there was something wrong with her that all these men kept trying to get in her pants. She would even wear layers of clothes to hide herself. So now she was paying attention to how men looked at her. She was scared that her mom's boyfriend would try next. Every so often, he would have that look in his eyes, so she made herself look more like a boy.

Do you have any idea that we put on countless masks for work, school, companions, guardians, kids, and so on that we fail to remember who we truly are? The regular day-to-day existence of being this way for this individual and that way for others that we genuinely neglect to focus on what our identity is and what we like since we would rather not put this and that in a bad mood, so we adjust our environmental elements.

What does the entirety of this truly mean? This can, in general, appear to be extremely obscure, except if we start to characterize ourselves. So, pause for a minute to recognize what your identity is. Who are you? There are many countless manners by which we characterize ourselves. We might display ourselves as our feelings (I'm stubborn, I'm meek, I'm serious), our callings (I'm a lawyer, I'm a specialist, I'm a student), our titles (I'm Chief VP), our salaries (I'm a tycoon), our jobs (I'm a mother, I'm the oldest of five young ladies), our ways of behaving (I'm a player), our assets (I'm a BMW proprietor), our illustrations (I'm big enchilada, I'm the low man on the command hierarchy), our input (I'm useless, I'm extraordinary), our otherworldly convictions (I'm Jewish), our looks (I'm delightful, I'm terrible, I'm old), our achievements (I'm the 1996 Homecoming Sovereign), our past (I'm a disappointment), and even what we're not (I'm not a slacker).

By the time Anonima turned 13, she had lost her virginity to a boy named Anthony. After she got her period, she started messing around with guys, but she would never let them stick it in. But on the day, she lost her virginity, she used a summer's eve douche so it wouldn't hurt, not knowing that it would make her dry and every time she attempted to have intercourse, the condom would get stuck and ripped apart. She waited all that time only to have the worst night of her life. After that, Anonima kept having sex with so many guys it became a game to her. She would sit and listen to how her brother and his friends talked about girls that she became just like them but made so they would be sitting by the phone waiting. She would always leave them hungry for more.

The character that our companions and friends have will, in general, influence us also. Look closely at your companions. Who you accept is, in many cases, an impression of who you accept you are. If your companions are exceptionally adoring, what's more, touchy, there's an extraordinary opportunity that you see yourself along these lines. The time period you use to characterize your personality is exceptionally strong too. Whether you shift focus over to your past, your present, or the future to characterize who you genuinely are. A long time back, my present and past weren't frightfully energizing, so I deliberately blended my character with the vision I had of who I realized I would turn into. I didn't need to pause; I started to live as this man now. It's important, when you are responding to this inquiry, to be in the right state. You really want to feel loose, safe, and inquisitive. If you're simply muscling through this book, filtering and perusing quickly, or on the other hand, if you have numerous interruptions, you won't find the solutions you really want. Take a deep, full breath in; loosen up the breath out. Allow your psyche to be interested — not unfortunate, not worried, not searching for flawlessness or for anything specifically. Simply ask yourself, "Who am I?"

Record the reply and afterward ask it once more. Each time you ask it, record whatever surfaces, and continue to test more profoundly and more profoundly. Keep on requesting until you find the depiction of yourself that you have the most grounded feeling about. How would you characterize yourself? What is the embodiment of 'what your identity is?' What similarities do you use to portray yourself? Which jobs do you play?

Frequently, if you don't make this protected and inquisitive expression, the feelings of terror in general and delays about personality will continue to offer you undersupplied responses. Truth be told, frequently, on the off chance that you simply pose this question in front of someone, proclaiming, "Who are you?" without placing them in the right state, you'll get one of two reactions:

Just as Anonima would put on her tight body suits and get the attention of her brothers' friends, they would sneak off to the basement and mess around and just tease them and claim that someone was coming, so they would have to stop. She became known for her teasing abilities. They would even offer her money to let them go all the way, so she would wait for the price to be right before she agreed. Every weekend and all through the summer, she would have a ball seducing them. Anonima had long hair and a body shaped like an hourglass. Although she was only 13, she was very smart and very mature for her age; all the boys were at least five years older. She noticed that her body was worth a lot to the guys, and she made it part of her hustle.

This kind of inquiry tosses many individuals into a spiral since they have never been called upon to genuinely consider what their response is. A superficial response. This is a first-endeavor avoidance procedure. This reaction can be characterized as the "Popeye Guideline," where an individual will essentially demand, "I'm what I am, and that is all that I am." Frequently, what I find is that when you pose somebody with a question, particularly a profound one, they won't reply to you until they've addressed two inquiries of their own. First, they ask themselves, "Could I at any point answer this question?" On the off chance that an individual doesn't know who he/she is, frequently they'll say, "I don't have the slightest idea," or offer you the primary surface response. At times people are hesitant to pose the question, understanding that they need clarity in this basic aspect of their lives. Also, the second question they ask themselves prior to nothing is: "How might this benefit me? If I answer this question, how might this benefit me actually?"

Allow me to offer you the solution to these two inquiries. To begin with, you, in all actuality, do know what your identity is. Indeed, you can come up with the response on the off chance that you pause for a minute to conceptualize a piece at the present time. Nevertheless, you must trust yourself to allow whatever responses to emerge from you and simply stream and record them on paper. Second, the advantage of knowing what your identity is, is the capacity to shape each of your ways of behaving immediately.

Chapter 5 - Pen and Paper Required

Quality inquiries make a quality life. They direct our psychological attentiveness and thus decide how we think and feel. The distinction in peoples' lives frequently boils down to the distinction in the questions they reliably pose to themselves. On the off chance that you ask a dis-engaging question (for example, "For what reason does this generally happen to me?"), your psychological PC will search for a response, regardless of whether it needs to make something up! It could formulate "In light of the fact that you're not kidding" and "In light of the fact that you don't have the right to do well in any case."

On the other hand, if you ask an engaging question, for example, "How might I take this experience and use it to add to other people?" Your cerebrum will search for replies to this question and frequently think of a response that will encourage you and can help other people, also.

The key is to foster an example of questions that empower you. The accompanying questions are intended to assist you in meeting more satisfaction, fervor, pride, appreciation, happiness, responsibility, and love your entire life. Think of a few responses for every one of these questions. Assuming you experience issues, basically, replace "am I" with the words "might I at any point be." For instance, "What might I be cheerful about in my life at this moment?" What am I most cheerful about in my life now? What might be said about that satisfies me? How does that make me feel?

What am I most amped up for in my life now? What might be said about that makes me invigorated? How does that cause me to feel? What am I most glad about in my life now? What might be said about that right by me? How does that cause me to feel? What am I most thankful for in my life now? What might be said that makes me appreciative? How does that cause me to feel? What do I appreciate most in my life at the present time? What do I appreciate? How does that make me feel? What am I dedicated to in my life at this moment? What can I say about what makes me committed? How does that make me feel? Who do I cherish? Who loves me? What might be said about that which I cherish? How does that cause me to feel? To make a change in your life, make this a piece of your everyday custom. By reliably asking these questions, you'll find that you access your most enabling close-to-home states consistently, and you'll start to make mental thruways to satisfaction, energy, pride, appreciation, euphoria, responsibility, and love. (Contribution to dating application)

Chapter 6 - What Is Character?

Everybody battles with existential questions, for example, "Who am I?" and "Who do I maintain that my future self should be?" One justification for this reason, might be that the response is so impressive.

Personality incorporates the numerous connections people develop, like their way of life as a youngster, companion, accomplice, and parent. It includes outside qualities over which an individual has next to zero control, like level, race, or financial class. Character likewise includes political suppositions, moral perspectives, and strict convictions, all of which guide the decisions one makes consistently.

Individuals who are excessively worried about the impression they make or who feel a central part of themselves, like orientation or sexuality, isn't being communicated can battle intensely with their character. Pondering the disparity between what one's identity is and who one needs to be can be a strong impetus for change.

Now around 13, Anonima would watch this guy and his family attend church, so she started dating him so that she could go with them. She always yearned for God in her life. So, she joined the church and kept going after they broke up. But it seems that although she got baptized in Jesus' name, she was filled with the holy ghost; there was a spirit that seemed to have attached itself to her, the spirit of promiscuity. No matter what she did or where she went, this spirit seemed to follow. She would catch a glimpse of herself in the mirror or on the reflection of a car, and she would see something that appeared like a shapeshift of good and evil that would be looking back at her. It was kind of like that movie, The Devil's Advocate, in 1997, where the wife, Mary Ann, would see fighting figures whose demons were showing their true self. That is a scary experience to see for yourself.

WHAT CHARACTERIZES PERSONALITY?

Personality includes the qualities individuals hold, which direct their decisions. A character contains various jobs — like a mother, educator, and U.S. resident — and every job holds importance and assumptions that are incorporated into one's personality. Character keeps on developing throughout the span of a singular's life.

HOW IS PERSONALITY SHAPED?

Character arrangement includes three key assignments: Finding and fostering one's true capacity, picking one's motivation throughout everyday life, and tracking down chances to practice that potential and reason. Character is additionally affected by guardians and companions during youth and trial and error in immaturity.

FOR WHAT REASON DON'T I GRASP MYSELF?

Everyone has an objective of supporting qualities and settling on decisions that are predictable to their actual self. Some assimilate the upsides of their families or culture, despite the fact that they don't line up with their credible selves. This contention can drive disappointment and vulnerability. Pondering one's qualities can ignite change and a seriously satisfying life.

WHAT IS A CHARACTER EMERGENCY?

The possibility of a character emergency rose out of clinician Erik Erikson, who depicted eight phases of emergencies and improvement, an idea later developed by others. Although not a clinical term, a personality emergency alludes to confronting a test of one's healthy identity, which might base on legislative issues, religion, vocation decisions, or orientation jobs.

A few years passed, and Anonima couldn't take all the fighting and arguing with her mom and boyfriend, so she ended up moving out on her own at age sixteen, where she became an independent minor and got an apartment for a nice price. All she had was her bed and clothes, so the pastor took her trash-picking in the nice neighborhoods to get a couch. She was so excited to finally have her own. So, one day she was in the shower, and she looked down only to find a hand reaching up out the drain. She screamed and hopped out of the shower, wondering how long these people had been watching her wash up. She was scared to leave the apartment by herself, fearing that they were watching her and could be planning to attack or rape her since they were bold enough to reach their hand up to grab her. A few days later, one of her friends came over, and they went to the landlord's office and demanded a refund. He refused, but after they mentioned calling the cops, he said he's been having trouble with the tenants that lived in the basement, that its 15 Mexican who refuse to leave. So she wouldn't be on the streets; he gave her two weeks to find another place; thankfully, she found a place on the 3rd floor, bigger and cheaper than what she had.

Struggling to make ends meet. Anonima had to drop out of school to get a full-time job. Anonima got hooked on the party line, she would have different guys coming in and out, and some she would have sex with just because she wanted them and the others for a fee. She would do anything to keep a roof over her head and not have to go back home. The bills had to be paid, and the job wasn't paying too much to a high-school dropout. Anonima was always looking for a quick buck; she couldn't stand being broke.

The party line got so busy, so she got the idea to create a safe meeting space free of judgment. A light bulb went off in her head; she could create a home diner, sell meals plus rent her bed out by the hour to have some extra income coming in. Word got out about the home diner, and she started generating a lot of business. She made up her mind to sleep with three more guys, and she would just focus on the diner.

When the first guy came, he had a gun, and he pointed it at her. She thought he was joking around, but then he cocked it back, and shit got real. He threatened to shoot her if she didn't do what he said. Anonima was terrified; she gave the best performance she could, anything to stay alive. He violated every part of her body, even sliding the cold steel inside her with his finger on the trigger. The sheets became saturated with blood. He must have known she had a change of heart and was ready to send him away. All she could do was pray; then, when he was done, he would never return. Anonima couldn't do anything or tell anyone because she felt like she had brought it on herself, and she had to accept her punishment for being greedy, just thankful that he let her live. Afterward, she shut down the party line and the home diner for fear of that happening again.

FOR WHAT REASON IS MY HIGH SCHOOLER CHANGING TO SUCH AN EXTENT?

Immaturity is a period where youngsters foster a genuine identity, particularly from their folks, to turn into free grown-ups. Trial and error are a significant piece of the cycle: As adolescents take a stab at various personalities — regarding companions, side interests, appearance, orientation, and sexuality — they come to understand what their identity is and who they need to be.

Chapter 7 - How Does Personality Impact Connections?

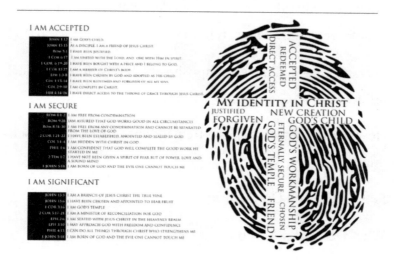

Elements of personality can feature likenesses or contrasts between individuals — through race, orientation, or calling — which can work to either join or partition. Individuals who view themselves as individuals from a bigger overall gathering will often have a more grounded connection with others, creatures, and nature.

Proverbs 23:7 reminds us:

"For as he thinks in his heart, so is he."

The battle for the mind begins with understanding who we are – our identity.

The Search for Our Identity

Socially – identify with race, gender, ethnicity, nationality, beliefs, economic status, religion.

Personally – skills, accomplishments, position, intellect, influence.

How we see ourselves has a tremendous impact on our self-image.

Perspectives on Our Identity.

What we do is not who we are.

A Rudderless Ship or a Real Purpose.

How we see ourselves controls us.

Losing the center that grounds us: serves "to magnify our general sense of uncertainty and, by association, fear, and anxiety" Not recognizing the source or giving it up leads to attachment to the world leads to "defining ourselves by virtue of things impermanent."

Impacts on Our Identity

Our background, our experiences, our temperament, and our training.

Key Question: Who are we deep inside – our true identity?

What God says about Our Identity "…count yourselves dead to sin but alive to God in Christ Jesus. Therefore, do not let sin reign in your mortal body so that you obey its evil desires." (Romans 6:11-12)

Not sinners saved by grace, but saints!

Chapter 8 - The Battle is First in Our Minds

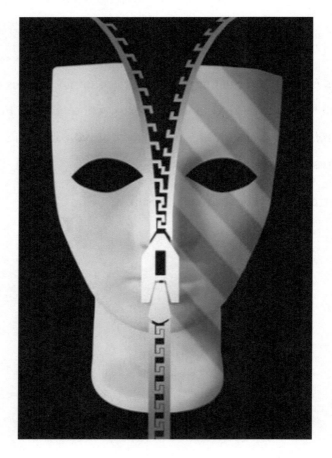

"Do not conform any longer to the pattern of this world but be transformed by the renewing of your mind." (Romans 12:2). The feelings (our heart), in the end, follow our choices (our head) to trust God to see ourselves as he sees us. Recharging Our Brains Science has found that we really can recharge our brains. We can see the expression of God to change our thought process, process data, and view ourselves.

Realizing God is critical to figuring out our actual identity.

We have four vital upsides of the congregation. They are (with no specific request); Realm Culture, His Presence, Family, and Character. Of the character, it states, "Realizing God is vital to figuring out our own personality and being OK with ourselves." I need to zero in on the initial segment of that assertion for one minute... "Realizing God is critical to understanding our own identity..." If we have any expectation of finding our actual identity, we should initially know God, the provider, everything being equal. It makes sense that an all-knowing God, our maker, would realize us far superior to what we know ourselves.

Jesus said in Matthew 7:24-27 (NIV), "Hence every individual who hears these expressions of mine and tries them resembles a shrewd man who constructed his home on the stone. The downpour descended, the streams rose, and the breezes blew and beat against that house; yet it didn't fall since it had its establishment on the stone. In any case, every individual who hears these expressions of mine and doesn't try them resembles a stupid man who fabricated his home on sand. The downpour descended, the streams rose, and the breezes blew and beat against that house, and it fell with an incredible accident."

Our identity in Christ is the foundation; it's a substantial piece that sits on top of the foundation. If we fail to understand the situation, it can subvert the entire house and would be like an earthquake altering your life.

There was a man who was stressed out because he struggled with his identity. He didn't know who he was or where he would end up. Robert acknowledged Jesus and began strolling in confidence; however, he never truly accepted he was excused for his past wrongs. Robert didn't consider himself to be an important part of God's family; that in some way, he was excluded from elegance and legacy.

Upon the arrival of Robert's sanctification, a voyaging evangelist (who had never met him) spoke prophetically to him during his lesson. Pinpointing the untruth, he had accepted, he started to pronounce his personality in God's loved ones. It was capably gotten at that point, yet tragically lost in time. Right up 'til now, Robert has left the confidence. I keep thinking about whether he had acknowledged these words and announced them as truth; he would have reproduced his personality and would, in any case, be following Christ today.

Who We Are in Christ

2 Corinthians 5:17-18 says, "Therefore, if anyone is in Christ, he is a new creation; the old has gone, the new has come!" God gives us a second chance; he cleans the record to begin new with him. He isn't simply fixing some of you, yet he is giving you a total makeover. "For you have been born again, not of perishable seed, but of imperishable, through the living and enduring word of God." (1 Peter 1:23-24)

Our Identity Crisis and God's Answer

Read and meditate on the word of God daily. Psalm 119:105 "Your word is a lamp to my feet and a light for my path." Pray for wisdom and understanding. James 1:5-6 "If any of you lacks wisdom, he should ask God, who gives generously to all without finding fault, and it will be given to him." Know God's power in you. 2 Peter 1:3-4 "His divine power has given us everything we need for life and godliness through our knowledge of him who called us by his own glory and goodness."

Fellowship with other Christians. Hebrews 10:25 "Let us not give up meeting together, as some are in the habit of doing, but let us encourage one another — and all the more as you see the day approaching."

Anonima learned her lesson; she knew she would never sell her body again. And she learned she needed to have protection, so she brought a gun, mace, brass knuckles, pockets, knives, and a taser. She moved to a new place, a house, and she was doing well until winter kicked in, and the gas bills started coming in almost 500 bucks. Burdened by the bills, and the rent was a lot more than the apartment. She decided to help her friends out by setting them up with random guys; since they were already doing it, why not profit from it? So Anonima would host private parties and would use the guest room as the boom-boom room, where the guys would pay only Anonima the money as agreed upon for the services rendered. Their IDs would be scanned, and they would be searched for weapons at the door. Drinks would be poured only by Anonima, and cash was paid in advance along with tips, and they were instructed never to speak of the payment rendered for service. After the deed was done, Anonima would provide the supplies she knew they needed, like picking up washers and dryers, diapers and clothes for their kids, and paying their bills, but she would never give them cash. Anonima did that for almost a year till the girls started getting sloppy and hooking up with them without her consent.

Chapter 9 - David and Goliath

Thinking about this subject of personality, I was drawn by the Holy Spirit to look at the tale of David and Goliath. You could understand the story well; however, have you at any point checked it out from the perspective of personality? I was floored by exactly the amount it radiates all through the story. Before we check out the sacred text, here's a rundown of the more extensive story for some specific situations.

David is a youthful shepherd who is getting things done for his dad between the family ranch and the Israelite armed force, which is positioned close by against the Philistines. Every day a monster Philistine hero named Goliath insults the Israelites and provokes them to a one-on-one duel to choose the fight. While all the Israelite warriors fall in dread, David chooses to make a move.

In 1 Samuel 17:41-45 (NIV), we read: "In the meantime, [Goliath], with his safeguard conveyor before him, continued to draw nearer to David. He looked David over and saw that he was minimal in excess of a kid, shining with well-being and attractive, and he loathed him. He told David, 'Am I a canine, that you come at me with sticks?' And the Philistine reviled David by his divine beings. 'Come here,' he said, 'and I'll give your tissue to the birds and the wild creatures!' David shared with the Philistine, 'You come against me with sword and lance and spear, yet I come against you for the sake of the Lord Almighty, the God of the armed forces of Israel, whom you have challenged.'"

Assuming you know all about the story, you'll realize what occurs straightaway. David routs Goliath in awesome design, and the term 'David and Goliath' lives on right up 'til now to become inseparable from the little man conquering difficulty to overcome the huge miscreant.

Chapter 10 - Your Character Is a Key Front Line

As recently expressed, your character is a key essential idea. It makes sense then that Satan, the "father of falsehoods," would need to annihilate it even more. A twisted, confounded, and mistaken character have to destroy outcomes for the entire, so we should know about the foe's plans.

In 1 Samuel 17:43 (NIV), Goliath tells David, "Am I a canine, that you come at me with sticks?" From the get-go, this could seem like honest ridiculing. Of the relative multitude of things Goliath might have shared with David, this appears to be genuinely harmless; however, there's something else to this besides what you could think.

Think about a stick with regard to this sacred writing. A stick is an innocuous plaything for a canine. It's a lifeless thing. Pointless. At any point been called futile? The foe frequently goes after our undertakings through self-uncertainty, calling us pointless, totally insufficient, and unfit every step of the way. It's one of his #1 affronts.

Presently we could anticipate this from the Goliaths of the world - an adversary who is effectively attempting to attack the triumph - yet what of our assumed partners? Believed loved ones who ought to be generally supporting us?

We could anticipate that the fight for our character should be at the cutting edge, yet it harms even more when it's from inside our own positions on the grounds that our safeguards are not amassed there. We don't necessarily, in every case, see it coming, and thus, it tends to undeniably more harm.

Prior to the story, David needs to persuade King Saul that he's qualified to battle Goliath. In 1 Samuel 17:33, Saul answers by saying, "You can't go out against this Philistine and battle him; you are just a young fellow, and he has been a champion from his childhood" (NIV). You could think this is all good. David was youthful, and his adversary, and Goliath, was at the pinnacle of his game.

In any case, there's more going on in the background. By this stage, Saul had a propensity for resisting God and chasing after his own needs and goals. He needed confidence. Our all-knowing God knew the result of the fight, and you get the sense He's hanging tight for somebody like David, a man apparently trying to win over His affections, to move forward and battle for Him.

As King of Israel, Saul ought to have been the one to confront Goliath, yet rather he endeavors to impede God's blessed substitution. In about one sentence, Saul, at the same time, subverts David's personality while advancing the adversary. David refers to him as "a young fellow." All in all, they were unpracticed, unfit, and frail. Of Goliath, there's just commendation, "...he has been a hero from his childhood". Saul is supporting the foe; it is a capable, perilous, world-class area of strength for and recommended Goliath.

I shiver to consider the vindictive things individuals have been called by their own alleged partners; their folks, kin, accomplices, or companions. The harm this can cause to an individual's personality can be destroyed. David answers the assaults by broadcasting what God's identity is and who he is in God and in deed.

In 1 Samuel 17:34-37 (NIV), David tells Saul, "Your worker has been keeping his dad's sheep. At the point when a lion or a bear came and stole away a sheep from the herd, I pursued it, struck it, and protected the sheep from its mouth. At the point when it turned on me, I held onto it by its hair, struck it, and killed it. Your worker has killed both the lion and the bear; this uncircumcised Philistine will be like one of them since he has resisted the militaries of the living God. The Lord who saved me from the paw of the lion and the paw of the bear will protect me from the hand of this Philistine. "At the end of the day, "I'm a lion slayer; I'm a bear slayer, and God will safeguard me."

We, in all actuality, do wealthy the equivalent when the foe attempts to subvert us by reaffirming what God's identity and we've had the option to accomplish through His adoration, elegance, and influence.

In 1 Samuel 17:38-39 (NIV), Saul, at last, allows David to battle Goliath. "Then Saul dressed David in his own tunic. He put a layer of reinforcement on him and a bronze cap on his head. David affixed his sword over the tunic and had a go at strolling around on the grounds that he was not used to them." Saul is attempting to make David into his rendition of a fighter by dressing him for the part. They were the two warriors; however, David didn't fit the conventional trooper form Saul was acclimated with. We're many times enticed to do the same by wearing a veil to become another person.

In all actuality, we are special and play various parts to play in this walk with Christ. Our singular abilities, gifts, interests, characters, and approaches are all important for our natural personality for His brilliance. The most debilitating action is claiming to be what you realize you're not. I really do express this with an alert, in any case, since I accept Satan involves this equivalent point for evil by distorting reality. It's generally offered to us with bogus slogans, for example, "conceived along these lines" or "be consistent with yourself."

These apparently honest assertions are frequently used to legitimize every kind of malevolent, likened to, "I'm naturally introduced to sin, and my inborn nature is shrewd. In this manner, I'm legitimate in my wrongdoing." It is clearly false, and individuals are misleading themselves with this mentality. Truly, all of us are on an excursion to turn out to be more Christlike. A few of us are called to be ministers, other evangelists, chairmen, and even needleworkers. Look into Dorcas in Acts 9. She had a straightforward service and did it persistently. She was certainly not a well-known evangelist or prophet, but her name sits with honor in the Bible.

Does this mean I excuse self-appraisal, fair study, and abstain from learning new open-talking strategies? Obviously not. I will adjust my techniques as I develop and improve for God's greatness. Eventually, be that as it may, I won't profess to be another person. God has gently sewn me together in my mom's belly to be me and a similar concern to you. Knowing our character in God is tremendously soothing in a fierce world.

In 1 Samuel 17:45-46, David tells Goliath, "You come against me with blade and lance and spear; however, I come against you for the sake of the Lord Almighty, the God of the militaries of Israel, whom you have resisted. This day the Lord will convey you into my hands, and I'll strike you down and cut off your head."

When did you last express that to Satan and his assaults? You can hear the certainty and confidence in the most natural sounding way for David, knowing what God's identity is and who he is in God. Our personality in God is unimaginably consoling. Through Him, we also can confront the Goliaths of our reality, standing firm against the tempests of life.

Chapter 11 - Our Undeniable Personality

Flicking through the Bible, we track down an abundance of consolation, pronouncing the idea of God and our character in Him. Did you realize the principal explanation concerning mankind found in the Bible is a personality-asserting statement? Beginning 1:27 says, "So God made humankind in his own picture, in the picture of God he made them; male and female he made them."

Did you hear that? You are not a mistake; the consequence of some irregular organic synthetic response.

Nor are you some plaything for an aloof god, disposed of like subterranean insects on this side of the world. No, you are super!

God Says We Are

Anonima and her many battles within; she set in her mind to set up an orgy with a few friends; after getting into an argument with her boyfriend, she battled with thoughts of women but was always trying to convince herself that she was strictly dickly. Today was going to be the day she was finally gonna be with a woman; she made all the arrangements and was waiting at the bus stop to get her freak on. One of her brothers saw her at the bus stop, and they all gathered around talking, so her brother Juan ran to the house to use the bathroom, and Anonima was talking with his wife Lucy when they noticed a car kept circling the block. Finally, Anonima noticed something flying their way, so she pushed her niece out of the way, and she jumped into what she thought was a firecracker since it was near the 4th of July.

Resting on the wall holding her stomach in shock, looking down at the drips of blood, she realized it wasn't a firecracker, but it was a bullet. She said a quick prayer asking God to forgive her, and at that moment, she felt gods hand reach in and pluck the bullet out! Her sister-in-law Lucy ran across the street to the house, yelling franticly; meanwhile, Anonima was still in shock because she knew what she felt, and she knew no one would believe her. Her mom ran to the medicine cabinet and got the gauze, and taped her up, and everyone rushed to the hospital. They took her back, prepping to remove the bullet, which was in the middle of her belly. The doctors were digging around looking for it, but they couldn't find it; no matter how many times she told them God plucked it out, no one believed her. They said the angle she was hit; should still be in there or exit out her back.

They gave their statement to the police, but Anonima was grateful that she protected her two years old niece because that bullet would have hit her right in the head. They packed the wound and wrapped her up, and sent her home. Soon as she got home, her boyfriend was waiting, scared that the last words they exchanged could be their last. The next Sunday, she shared her full testimony with the church confessing her sins before the congregation, just thanking God for his grace and mercy, and forgiveness.

1 John 3:1 "How great is the love the Father has lavished on us, that we should be called children of God! And that is what we are!" In a position of high privilege –

His children Galatians 5:1 "It is for freedom that Christ has set us free." (John 8:36) "So if the Son sets you free, you will be free indeed." Liberated from transgression's stranglehold. 1 Corinthians 6:19-20 "Do you not know that your body is a temple of the Holy Spirit, who is in you, whom you have received from God? You are not your own; you were bought at a price. Therefore, honor God with your body." His asylum, His abode. Colossians 1:13-14 "For he has rescued us from the dominion of darkness and brought us into the kingdom of the Son he loves, in whom we have redemption, the forgiveness of sins." Moved out of murkiness and into His realm. Philippians 3:20 "But our citizenship is in heaven. And we eagerly await a Savior from there, the Lord Jesus Christ,"

Citizens of His Kingdom, not this world. Romans 8:38-39 "For I am convinced that neither death nor life, neither angels nor demons, neither the present nor the future, nor any powers, neither height nor depth, nor anything else in all creation, will be able to separate us from the love of God that is in Christ Jesus our Lord." Can't be separated from Christ. 2 Corinthians 5:18,20 "All this is from God, who reconciled us to himself through Christ and gave us the ministry of reconciliation, ... We are therefore Christ's ambassadors," Reconciled with Him and His ministers of reconciliation.

God says collectively we are one Peter 2:9-10 "But you are a chosen people, a royal priesthood, a holy nation, a people belonging to God, that you may declare the praises of him who called you out of darkness into his wonderful light. Once you were not a people, but now you are the people of God;" His people called for His purpose, and we are stronger together.

Win the Fight for Your Mind.

Know your identity in Christ.

Expand your spiritual influence on Him.

Live in your real purpose.

Today, I accept our inherent character is enduring an onslaught. We even instruct our children at school that they are just creatures tearing through space on this cluster of soil we call Earth. All things considered, that's what I trust; assuming you tell somebody they're just a creature sufficiently long, they'll ultimately begin behaving like one. Try not to trust that falsehood. Your actual character is tracked down in God, our magnificent Father.

Anonima had a friend who experienced occasional episodes of gloom. He was so exasperated with his psychological well-being battles he tossed down his digging tool out of frustration, set a straight shot for the skyline, and took off to pass on. He made no arrangements. No food. No water. Allow me to guarantee you that in these hot and dry circumstances, you won't keep going long. As he strolled, he shook his clenched hand at the sky, yelling, "God! You made me think along these lines. I'm broke. I was made off-base."

He, in the end, showed up at the coast and tested God (I don't suggest you do this - Deuteronomy 6:16 and Luke 4:12), saying, "Assuming you truly love me, you'd save me." At that exact second, he saw a plastic jug weaving in the sea. He swam out to gather it and was adequately sure that it was brimming with new water. As he drank, God talked significantly to him, "You are valuable to me. I love you, and I have an expectation and a future for you."

From that second on, he is not entirely set in stone to make do, at last getting back to civilization to share his experience. Regardless of what your identity is or where you've been, nothing absolves you from your actual character tracked down in Jesus.

What Is Personality?

There is far-reaching research on a character that demonstrates the way that character improvement can be a troublesome or wild period in an individual's life. Erik Erikson, a significant figure in personality research, hypothesized that we as a whole go through phases of psychosocial improvement during the lives that challenge us to create certain skills.

That's what Erikson recommends if you don't accomplish the capacity to lay out character or job inside society and yourself, this stage can welcome a personality emergency (additionally called "job disarray"). On the off chance that you feel constrained in a personality, you might start to rebel, experience misery, and even make a pessimistic form of yourself.

Concerns Like a Character Emergency

A character emergency can, at times, be a more broad and unclear term used to depict quite a few testing circumstances. By and by, you may be encountering a character emergency, or it very well may be:

- Emotional meltdown

- Quarter life emergency
- Vocational changes or disappointment
- Orientation dysphoria
- Change jumble
- An emotional well-being problem like sadness or bipolar issue
- Indications of a Personality Emergency

A personality emergency might cause sensations of dissatisfaction, being stuck, or lacking significant movement. Besides, a character emergency can impact sensations of sorrow or nervousness, causing individuals to feel unsatisfied with themselves and their lives. This kind of private emergency might be harder to recognize in one's own self as the experience is more unclear than the side effects of other psychological wellness sicknesses.

Here are normal indications of a personality crisis:

Scrutinizing your personality.

Addressing qualities that impact your self-insight.

Scrutinizing your motivation or energy throughout everyday life.

Encountering tension or distress.

Modifying your qualities or tendencies habitually to match your current circumstance or relationship.

Trouble addressing inquiries concerning yourself.

Trouble confiding in your capacity to simply decide is It Something More Serious?

A personality emergency can be a tricky and awkward circumstance; however, it isn't normally risky. Something different can fill the character emergency and result in a more difficult circumstance - wretchedness. Wretchedness is a general term for a gathering of burdensome temperament problems that lead to low mind-set. It can likewise prompt self-hurt, considerations of death, and self-destruction.

Indications of sorrow might include:

- Mind-set changes and peevishness
- Low energy and inspiration
- Loss of interest in pleasurable exercises
- Rest, craving, or weight changes
- Unfortunate consideration, fixation, and direction
- Considerations about death and kicking the bucket
- Feeling accelerated or dialed back

How Character Creates

Character creates as an individual advance through various situations. Contingent upon an individual's status, they could be investigating another personality or holding solid to their present status.

The four sorts of personality status include Dispossession: An individual in dispossession is firmly dedicated to their perspectives, yet they have needed investigation. Frequently, they adhere to the point of view others spread out for them.

Accomplishment: On the other hand, individuals in the accomplishment status had an exploratory meeting prior to settling on their character. They commit to responsibilities considering their own convictions and values.

Dispersion: In dissemination, individuals are deficient with regard to responsibility in their lives. More regrettably, they are not pursuing a condition of responsibility.

Ban: These individuals are the searchers. They are attempting to track down their personality and are exploring different avenues regarding choices prior to committing completely.

Reasons for a Character Emergency. Many reasons for character emergencies are genuinely normal and incorporate large life-altering events, stress, or general progression through the various phases of life.

Relationship changes (heartfelt, amicable, or familial) These causes can influence your capability on an essential level. They might try and be a shock, influencing your viewpoint of yourself, as well as your viewpoints on your occupation, connections, values, and interests.

Personality Emergencies in Teenagers additionally will often be less acquainted with procedures used to adapt to horrendous accidents, misfortunes, and changes in connections, which expands their gamble for pressure and uneasiness. While the advancement of self-esteem is unimaginably significant for youths as they start on the excursion to self-revelation, individuals at any stage in life are in danger of encountering a character emergency.

Is a Character Emergency Something worth being thankful for? An emergency might seem like a clearly regrettable circumstance; however, it may not be totally negative. Personality emergencies offer individuals the chance to investigate elective perspectives, feelings, and living. Character emergencies can act as an advance notice framework to demonstrate that there's an issue. By perceiving the issue, the individual can address and determine the issue. Ideally, the outcome is a more joyful, better person who is all the firmer on their character and their qualities.

Chapter 12 - Ways to Adapt to a Personality Emergency

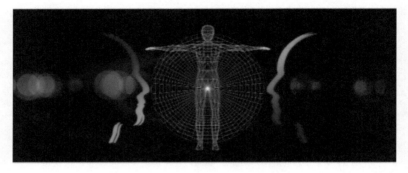

While a personality emergency can be hard to deal with, it is a typical encounter, and there are ways of adapting, like rehearsing objectivity, testing pessimistic considerations, and getting some margin to communicate your qualities, wants, and needs. Adapting to a character emergency expects you to search internally and do some investigation of yourself without interior or outside judgment.

Practice objectivity: Permit yourself an opportunity to reflect prior to responding. Challenge negative and nonsensical considerations: Have an impact on the way you see tough spots and occasions and any regrettable self-talk, and permit time to recognize what is making you self-conscious. Communicate your thoughts: Work on conveying the qualities that mean a lot to you. Participate in directed contemplations or journaling: Effectively reflect and cycle to decrease any likely nervousness and increment mindfulness. Participate in taking care of oneself: Work toward expanded self-acknowledgment and mindfulness. Distinguish novel qualities in yourself: Increment mindfulness and information on how you need to invest your energy pushing ahead. Figure out how to define limits: While attempting to sort out what your identity is and what you deeply desire, defining limits with individuals and responsibilities can assist you with clearing things out.

Stay away from pessimistic adapting: Emergencies might be awkward, and many individuals utilize negative adapting abilities to get away or stay away from uneasiness. Make sure to keep away from medications, liquor, and indiscriminate sex and spotlight your personality. Incline toward the emergency: Remaining on the thought, assemble solace in presenting yourself to the emergency. It might have an unnerving name; however, you can restrict the inconvenience by managing it straightforwardly, with trustworthiness and receptiveness. Keep future-situated: Pondering what's to come sets you in a superior position. The cycle might be troublesome now; however, it permits you to improve as a cheerful individual later in life.

Chapter 13 - Review

What is self-identity?

In this section, you can track down a few reciprocals, antonyms, everyday explanations, and related words for self-identity, like confidence, selfhood, self-sorting out, personhood, individual character, collectivity, subjectivity, self-definition, separateness, sociality.

What is social identity?

Social personality alludes to the manners in which that individuals' self-ideas depend on their participation in gatherings. Models incorporate games groups, religions, identities, occupations, sexual direction, ethnic gatherings, and orientation.

What variables make up your personality?

Personality development and advancement are influenced by different inside and outside factors like society, family, friends and family, nationality, race, culture, area, amazing open doors, media, interests, appearance, self-articulation, and educational encounters.

Conflicting personality psychosis (recently known as a different behavioral condition) is believed to be a complex mental condition that is logically brought about by many variables, including serious injury during youth (normally outrageous, tedious physical, sexual, or psychological mistreatment).

What Is Conflicting personality psychosis?

Conflicting personality psychosis is a serious type of separation, a psychological cycle that creates an absence of association in an individual's considerations, recollections, sentiments, activities, or feelings of the character. Conflicting personality psychosis is remembered to originate from a blend of variables that might incorporate injury experienced by the individual with the problem. The dissociative viewpoint is believed to be a survival technique - the individual, in a real sense, turns down or separates themselves from a circumstance or experience that is excessively rough, horrible, or excruciating to acclimatize with their cognizant self.

Who Is In danger of (DID) dissociative identity disorder?

Research shows that the reason for (DID) is a logical mental reaction to relational and natural burdens, especially during youth years when close-to-home disregard or manhandling may disrupt character improvement. As numerous as most people who foster dissociative issues have perceived individual chronicles of repeating, overwhelming, and frequently perilous unsettling influences or injuries at a delicate formative phase of experience growing up (for the most part before age 6).

Separation may likewise happen when there has been relentless disregard or psychological mistreatment, in any event, when there has been no obvious physical or sexual maltreatment. Discoveries show that in families where guardians are alarming and flighty, the youngsters might become dissociative. Studies demonstrate (DID) influences around 1% of the populace. Step-by-step instructions to Perceive Conflicting personality psychosis and Its Related Mental Issues.

Conflicting personality psychosis is described by the presence of at least two particular or split characters or characters expresses that consistently have control over the individual's way of behaving. With conflicting personality psychosis, there's additionally powerlessness to review key individual data that is excessively far coming to be made sense of as simple absent-mindedness. With conflicting personality psychosis, there are likewise profoundly particular memory varieties that might change. Albeit not every person encounters (DID) in a similar way, for some, the "changes" or various characters have their own age, sex, or race. Every person has their own stances, signals, and unmistakable approach to talking. Occasionally the modifies are nonexistent individuals; in some cases, they are creatures. As every character uncovers itself and controls the people's way of behaving and contemplations, it's designated "exchanging." Exchanging can require seconds to minutes to days. Some look for treatment with spellbinding where the individual's unique "modifies" or characters might be exceptionally receptive to the advisor's solicitations.

Different side effects of conflicting personality psychosis might incorporate cerebral pain, amnesia, time misfortune, dazes, and "otherworldly encounters." Certain individuals with dissociative problems have an inclination toward self-mistreatment, destructive behavior, and even savagery (both self-incurred and ostensibly coordinated). For instance, somebody with conflicting personality psychosis might end up doing things they wouldn't regularly do, like speeding, crazy driving, or taking cash from their boss or companion, yet they feel a sense of urgency to make it happen. Some depict this inclination as a traveler in their body as opposed to the driver. All in all, they genuinely accept they must choose between limited options.

There are a few primary ways by which the mental cycles of conflicting personality psychosis fundamentally have an impact on the way individual encounters living, including the accompanying:

Depersonalization. This is a feeling of being segregated from one's body and is frequently alluded to as an "unexplainable" experience. Derealization. This is the inclination that the world isn't genuine or looking hazy or distant.

Amnesia. This is the inability to review critical individual data that is so broad it can't be accused of common distraction. There can likewise be miniature amnesias where the conversation participated in isn't recollected, or the substance of a significant discussion is forgotten over time.

Character disarray or personality change. Both include a feeling of disarray about who an individual is. An illustration of character disarray is the point at which an individual has trouble characterizing the things that interest them throughout everyday life, or their political or strict or social perspectives, their sexual direction, or their expert desires. Notwithstanding these clear modifications, the individual might encounter mutilations in time, spot, and circumstance.

It is currently recognized that these separated states are not completely mature characters, but instead, they address an incoherent feeling of personality. With amnesia usually connected with conflicting personality psychosis, different character states recollect various parts of self-portraying data. There is generally a "have" character inside the person who relates to the individual's genuine name. Amusingly, the host character is typically ignorant about the presence of different characters.

Looking back at the adventures and curveballs Anonima encountered, what do you think about her character? Can you relate? Are you able to identify her crisis situations? Anonima had a battle within her mind and body all day. She struggled with her sexuality. She hated that she was born a woman; she felt like she was supposed to be a man, and she had penis envy. Anonima thought about having a sex change, but when she found out the size of the penis she would get, and how they do the procedure, she changed her mind; it wasn't worth it. She spent the next two decades as a lesbian.

Anonima changed her name to Atticus, and so for sixteen of those years, she dressed like a guy and acted like one. She was the man in all her relationships; she even married a woman who lasted five years. She became a foster parent, which was a little confusing to the kids when she would explain what to call her. Her life was an emotional roller-coaster. Are you wondering whether she became a lesbian because of all the experiences she had with men? She went from one extreme to another.

Chapter 14 – Gender Identity

Individuals with orientation dysphoria might have a scope of sentiments and ways of behaving that show uneasiness or misery. The degree of trouble can be extreme and influence all parts of their life. Indications of orientation dysphoria in kids. The conclusion of orientation dysphoria in youth is uncommon.

Most kids who appear to be confounded about their orientation character when youthful won't keep on feeling the same far past pubescence. Pretending is normal in small kids. In any case, inquire as to whether you are concerned your kid is giving indications of being discouraged, restless or removed. You should inquire as to whether these ways of behaving have been seen at school prior to looking for guidance.

Indications of orientation dysphoria in young people and grown-ups. If your sensations of orientation dysphoria started in youth, you might now have a much clearer feeling of your orientation character and how you need to manage it. In any case, you may likewise figure out that the sentiments you had at a younger age vanish after some time, and you feel quiet with your organic sex.

Or on the other hand, you might find yourself identifying as gay, lesbian, or sexually unbiased.

The way orientation dysphoria influences young people and grown-ups is different for kids. You might feel sure that your orientation personality clashes with your organic sex agreeable just when in the orientation job of your favored orientation personality (may incorporate non-double), a powerful urge to stow away or be freed of actual indications of your natural sex, like bosoms or beard growth a solid abhorrence of the private parts of your natural sex.

You might feel lonely or detached from others. You may likewise confront tension from companions, colleagues or coworkers, or family to act with a specific goal in mind. Or then again, you might confront tormenting and provocation for being unique. Having or smothering these sentiments influences your profound mental prosperity.

Because of sensations of misery and disgrace, numerous people with orientation dysphoria become socially disconnected — whether by decision or through shunning — which can add to low confidence and may prompt school revolution or, in any event, exiting.

At times of orientation dysphoria, the unsettling influence can be inescapable to such an extent that a person's psychological life spins around exercises that decrease orientation-related trouble. These people might be engrossed with their appearance, particularly preceding or from the get-go in a conventional orientation change. Associations with relatives may likewise be genuinely hindered, especially in situations where relatives hold negative or defaming sees about transsexual or orientation-non-adjusting people.

Those with orientation dysphoria tragically experience substance-related messes, self-destructive ideation, and self-destruction endeavors more usually than those everybody. After orientation change happens, self-destruction hazard might disseminate or persevere, contingent upon the change of the person. Kids with orientation dysphoria might show existing together fear of abandonment, summed up uneasiness, confusion, or side effects of gloom. Grown-ups may show tension and burdensome side effects too.

Orientation dysphoria has been accounted for across numerous nations and societies, and incongruences between sex and orientation have existed in human culture for millennia. The degree of misery experienced by somebody with orientation dysphoria can be huge, and people improve assuming they are in steady conditions, permitted to communicate their orientation in the way that is generally agreeable to them, and are given information that, if vital, medicines exist to decrease the feeling of incongruence they feel.

The reasons for orientation dysphoria are at present obscure; however, qualities, hormonal impacts in the belly, and natural variables are completely thought to be involved.

The beginning of cross-orientation interests and exercises is, as a rule, between ages 2 and 4 years, and many guardians later report that their youngster has consistently had cross-orientation interests. Just a few kids with orientation dysphoria will keep on having side effects in later puberty or adulthood. Normally, kids with orientation dysphoria are alluded to around the hour of the school section, especially assuming companion connections become testing or guardians suspect that their youngster's orientation character issues are not a stage.

The grown-up beginning is ordinarily ahead of schedule to mid-adulthood. There are two familiar courses for the improvement of orientation dysphoria: The first, commonly seen in late youth or adulthood, is a continuation of orientation dysphoria that had a beginning in adolescence or early puberty. Some have indications of cross-orientation, and it shows up later in mid-adulthood.

Chapter 15 - Step-by-step instructions to be consistent with yourself

POSITIVE PEERS 4 HIV CARES

However, it's not difficult to discuss how to be consistent with yourself; it can really be a provoking choice to make and finish. This implies standing tall with your viewpoints and considerations, protecting them, and not allowing yourself to slide into an assessment since its famous or acknowledged.

This takes boldness; however, truly, it's such a ton simpler acting naturally and remaining consistent with you than it is professing to be another person. However, since you're here, you know that now is the ideal time to roll out an improvement and carry on with your daily routine the way you need to experience it.

The most effective method is to be consistent with yourself.

Assuming you understand this, you're, as of now, at the limit. You're worn out on paying attention to what every other person maintains that you should do, say, or be. You followed the thoughts and assessments of others for quite a long time, in any event, when you disagreed with them. What's going on with that? Obviously, this is associated with your confidence and dread. We, as a whole, battle with these issues, so you're not alone.

Perhaps you discuss individuals acting truly; at the same time, we should get genuine; you're not being valid and authentic by the same token. Thus, you feed this endless loop of phoniness. You're becoming weary of it, right? Why burn through your time being false to yourself when you can figure out how to be consistent with yourself?

#1 Quit being a sheep. Stop and think for a minute; a large portion of us try not to be consistent with ourselves since we need to be loved. We're frightened that our perspectives will drive others away, and being hated is not a decent inclination; we know that. So, all things considered, we transformed into accommodating people.

If you have any desire to be consistent with yourself, quit being a sheep and attempt to be kind. Figure out how to adore and satisfy yourself as well as other people will follow.

Beginning saying "no." Goodness, I realize that this is a hard one. It's difficult to say "no" to individuals we care about and put down sound stopping points. Normally, we say "OK" to individuals since we would rather not frustrate others.

Be that as it may, generosity doesn't make you a legend; it simply implies you put your requirements behind others. That is not self-esteem. This doesn't mean you want to say "no" with outrage or sharpness; simply say "no" deferentially and solidly.

Focus on yourself. It's so natural to become involved with others' fantasies, objectives, and plans. In any case, this is your life; it's not intended to be utilized to ensure others accomplish their fantasies. Plunk down with yourself and investigate your fantasies, objectives, and plan.

What are the things you need to achieve in your life? Put forth reasonable and little objectives to assist you with accomplishing your own fantasies.

Eliminate poisonous individuals from your life. Okay, indeed, the poisonous ones. These are the ones that you generally help, yet they never support your objectives or are apathetic regarding them. If you have any desire to remain consistent with yourself, eliminate individuals who judge you. You lack the opportunity and willpower to manage them. Regardless, they just bring interruptions. Encircle yourself with individuals who love the individual you are.

Get profound. On the off chance that you're not consistent with yourself, you don't interface with yourself on a close-to-home level. You continually push down your genuine sentiments to seem a specific way; however, it's every one-off an untruth. Now is the right time to get genuine with yourself. Carry the secret feelings to the surface. Anything that you feel where it counts bring it out. Now is the right time.

Assume a sense of ownership of your life. Nobody constrained you to place yourself in the last spot. It was brought about by low confidence. Yet presently, it is the ideal time to recognize it and work on it. No other person will help you on the off chance that you're not able to help yourself. Thus, assume a sense of ownership of your life and own it. The past is previously; presently you just have the future in front of you.

You are what your identity is. You can attempt to be whoever else you need to be; however, by the day's end, it's all bologna. To be consistent with yourself, you must acknowledge what your identity is. If not, you can never find bliss since you're phony; carry on with your own life. Trust me; she's simply a result of the business.

You will kick the bucket. This is the main way I can say this. In the long run, at some point, your life will be finished. Recall that. Realizing that your life will end sooner or later, how could you not pursue your fantasies and be consistent with yourself? Genuinely carry on with the existence you need by being you.

Understand what your assets are. You might feel that you should be another person since you're not sufficient, and so on, yet you are. Everybody has their assets and shortcomings. You center around your shortcomings instead of your assets. Take a gander at what your assets are and center around them.

You will commit errors. Stop and think for a minute; you will screw up a route. There will be minutes where you will re-think if this is smart; however, tune in; this is only a little obstacle. Do you believe being veritable and genuine is simple? Damnation no! Individuals can't stand that since the greater part of them can't be authentic and fair themselves.

Resist the urge to stress about yourself. This isn't something present moment; this will be a cycle that will last a long time. Changing your confidence is a drawn-out project that you continually fight with. Toward the end, it merits the battle. Be that as it may, meanwhile, don't challenge yourself. You will have highs and lows. It's simply a piece of life.

Being okay is going. You've proactively hit this point in your life where you're worn out on being another person and following others. Along these lines, you made it past one monster impediment. Monitoring the issue is a colossal step, and you've leaped over it. From now on, it'll be a test; however, nothing you can't achieve.

After those two decades, Anonima found her way back to God and reestablished her foundation; she removed herself from her past life to begin with, a new slate, a blank canvas. Anonima is back in church and living for God, with hopes of finding a husband when God sees fit. Don't think you're stuck in any situation or circumstance. You can start over, wipe the slate clean and recreate the new you. Be true to yourself, and the rest will fall in place. Let's strengthen our character together!

Understanding Your Emotions/Feelings

Here is a list of emotions you can use to understand and describe how you feel:

LIST OF FEELINGS

- woe
- weary
- weariness
- vigilance
- tranquil
- torment
- stoical
- stingy

- vigilance
- tranquil
- torment
- stoical
- stingy
- spite
- timidity
- thrill

- sympathy
- watchfulness
- wary
- vivacious
- surprise
- suffering
- pessimism
- pensive

- sad
- roused
- revulsion
- self-assured
- scorn
- resigned
- remorse
- rapture

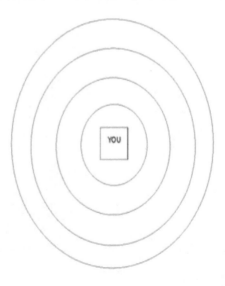

YOU

Angry	Negative	Uneasy
Amused	Disgust	Embarrassment
Annoyed	Furious	Livid
Bossy	Manipulative	Cocky
Disdainful	Bitter	Stupid
Eager	Loving	Receptive
Elated	Excited	Content
Fatherly	Player	Procrastinator
Flat	Apathetic	Weak
Forgiving	Hopeful	Motivated
Frightened	Happy	Positive
Frustrated	cross	Irritated
Heartbroken	Abandoned	Awe
Hurt	Inadequate	Trapped
Indifferent	Mixed-up	Foolish
Insecure	Cross	Confused
Inspired	Daring	Energetic
Kind	Giving	Sarcastic
Lonely	Shocked	Disconnected
Nervous	Tense	Flustered
Opinionated	Silly	Gorgeous
Pain	Adoration	Passionate
Petrified	Threatened	Horrified
Pleased	Glad	Wonderful
Satisfied	Confident	Determined
Spoiled	Selfish	Generous
Stubborn	Spoiled	Motherly
Surprised	Proud	Relieved
Sympathetic	Ecstatic	Cautious
Tired	Scared	Distrustful

This is just an example of how you can do your will, but I really would like you to do the exercise and fill your choice with descriptive words that make you who you are as a whole. Then, we will break it down into three categories of the Good| Bad\Indifferent.

Now we all go by different names; sometimes we call them our alter egos... So, what I would like you to do is name your alter ego, also known as your scapegoat. Some of you might have more than one. Don't be shy about bringing them to the surface.

Some of the links that might help are:

enragedhttps://www.professional-counselling.com/anger-management-tips.html

signshttps://www.professional-counselling.com/your-husband-or-wife-is-cheating.html

scornfulhttps://www.professional-counselling.com/emotional-abuse-signs.html

shamehttps://www.professional-counselling.com/how-to-deal-with-toxic-shame.html

worthlesshttps://www.professional-counselling.com/how-to-build-self-esteem.html

anxioushttps://www.professional-counselling.com/anxiety-for-no-reason.html

angryhttps://www.professional-counselling.com/anger-management-counseling.html

boredhttps://www.professional-counselling.com/bored-with-life.html

anxioushttps://www.professional-counselling.com/anxiety-for-no-reason.html

trappedhttps://www.professional-counselling.com/signs-your-husband-or-wife-wants-to-leave-you.html

inadequatehttps://www.professional-counselling.com/how-to-build-self-esteem.html

miserablehttps://www.professional-counselling.com/depression-help-online.html

nervoushttps://www.professional-counselling.com/anxiety-for-no-reason.html

uneasyhttps://www.professional-counselling.com/stressed-for-no-reason.html

trappedhttps://www.professional-counselling.com/signs-of-an-abusive-relationship.html

The Emotion Wheel

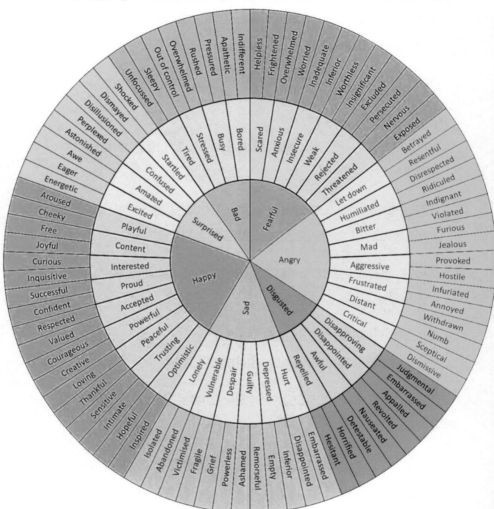

Sources

The King James Holy Bible

National Alliance on Mental Illness: "Dissociative Identity Disorder."

Erikson, E.H. (1968). Identity: youth and crisis. Norton & Co.

Erikson, E. H. (1980). Identity and the life cycle. W W Norton & Co.

Psychology Today Magazines

About the Author

Davon Hubbard is a brilliant author, mentor and advocate. She has devoted many years of her life to education and vindicating for elderly, disabled and troubled youth.

Davon enjoys traveling, bowling and spending time with family and friends. Her approach to living a balanced life has helped so many families and couples redeem severed relationships through mediation, interactive games, and communication.

Davon incorporates life experiences and her educational background in business and psychology to present her book in a transparent and real way that is sure to resonate with its readers. "True Identity", brings awareness to the toxic cycles of life that has crippled so many.

"True Identity" challenges its readers to push past pain and trauma and equips them with useful tools to become the best version of themselves, thus finding our "True Identity."

Made in the USA
Columbia, SC
02 March 2025